THE HERITAGE COLLECTION

THE GIRL WHO BECAME PRESIDENT:
ELLEN JOHNSON SIRLEAF

ROSEMOND SARPONG OWENS

ILLUSTRATED BY SKYE BROOKSHIRE

Lion's Historian PRESS
Amplifying Authentic Voices

The Girl Who Became President: Ellen Johnson Sirleaf

Copyright © 2022 by Rosemond Sarpong Owens

Illustrator: Skye Brookshire

Layout designer: Nasim Malik Sarkar

Library of Congress Control Number: 2022900875

All rights reserved.

No part of this publication may be reproduced, stored in a retrieval system, a database and/or published in any form or by any means, electronic, mechanical, photocopying, recording or otherwise, without the prior written permission of the publisher.

ISBN: 978-1-956051-16-2 (hardcover)

Published by Lion's Historian Press
https://www.lionshistorian.net/

Map of Liberia

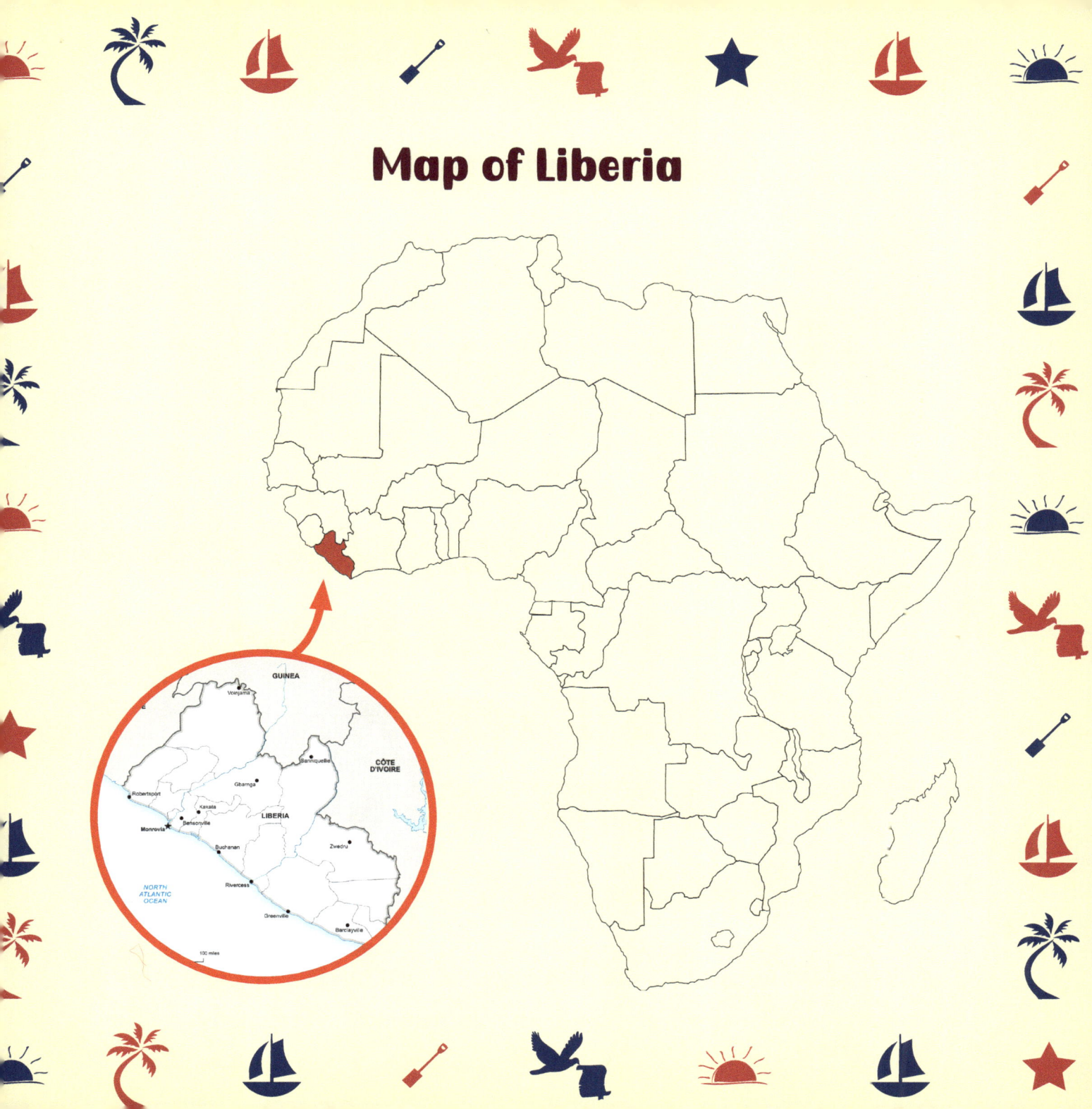

The Liberian National Flag

The Liberian national flag is called the "Lone Star." The eleven horizontal stripes represent the eleven signers of the declaration of independence, and the constitution of the Republic of Liberia; the blue field symbolizes the continent of Africa; the five-pointed white star depicts Liberia as the first "independent republic" on the continent of Africa; the red color designates "valor," the white, "purity;" and the blue, "fidelity." Although these representations are uniquely Liberian, the flag itself is a replica of "Old Glory," the national flag of the United States.

The Seal of Liberia (Coat of Arms)

The national seal consists of a palm tree representing the natural resources of Liberia, the plow and spade which illustrate the means of developing those resources, a dove with a scroll, which represents communication, and living in peaceful coexistence with other nations, the emerging sun, which represents the birth of Liberia, a sailing ship representing arriving settlers, and the motto "The Love of Liberty Brought Us Here" which represents the wishes, dreams, and hopes of arriving settlers.

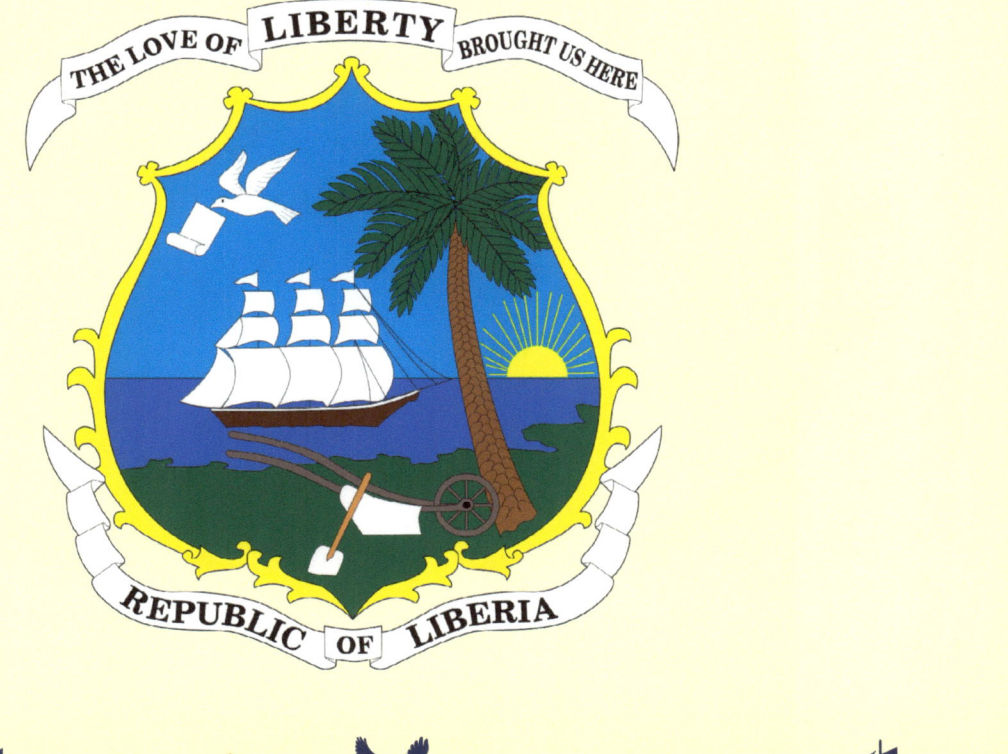

Dedication

To girls who dare to become leaders and changemakers.

Editorial Review

Everything that is created comes from a dream. Dreams build nations, families and individuals. Once a person has a dream, they have to believe that it can become a reality, and then begin to work towards making that dream come true.

Dreams come to both girls and boys, and women and men alike. This process is used by the Almighty God to show each of us what he has created each of us for. Some who dream do not pay attention to the message in their dreams. Others who dream forget the dreams. But others dream, wake up, believe that it can become a reality and work towards it.

This is the story of *The Girl Who Became President*.

At an early age, she had a dream that one day she would become the president of her nation. In those early days, there were no female leaders across the world, perhaps only the Queen of England. But the dream left a message in her spirit that God created everyone equal; and that each one could be whatever they dreamed. So the little girl went about her life planning and preparing and achieving great things. She allowed nothing to stand in her way of the dream she had seen. There were good days, and sad days, and tough days and difficult days; yet she kept moving forward towards her goal. She never got tired or discouraged or defeated, she used every obstacle placed in her way as a stepping stone to the next level; she used every wrong word thrown at her as a reminder to keep walking towards her goal; she used every deception thrown in her way to learn new lessons about human beings, to understand and know how to navigate the road of life. At the end, she climbed up to the mountain top of her dreams; and became the first democratically elected female president of Africa.

This book takes one through the process and gives lessons of dreams, perseverance, commitment, and success - if only you can believe that all things are possible.

Yes indeed I can resound, that all things are possible if you can dream it, believe it, work towards it, and achieve it.

It is possible.

— **Her Excellency Jewel Taylor**
Vice President of Liberia

Contents

The Beginning 1

Growing up in Liberia 3

Education is Key 5

Getting Married and Starting a Family 7

Going to America 9

Return to America and Back 11

Life of Service in Government 13

The Civil Wars 15

Route to Becoming President 17

Madam President 19

Accomplishments 21

Ellen's Work Continues 23

About the Author 24

References 25

Acknowledgements 26

Other Books in the Heritage Collection 27

Chapter 1

The Beginning

The country of Liberia was founded in the 19th century by freed slaves from the United States. Ellen Eugenia Johnson was born in its capital, Monrovia, on October 29, 1938. Ellen's father, Jahmele Carney Johnson, and her mother, Martha Dunbar, rejoiced greatly at her birth. Ellen was the couple's third child, preceded by her brother, Charles, and her sister, Jennie.

As is the custom in Liberia, a few days after Ellen was born, a wise old man came to Ellen's home to offer his good wishes. He looked at Ellen and said, "This child shall be great. This child is going to lead."

> The Monrovia of today is a grand but wounded city, the bruised and battered capital of a bruised and battered land. The Monrovia of my youth was a different place: simpler in feel, smaller in scale. We loved it dearly.

Chapter 2

Growing up in Liberia

Ellen's mother was an English teacher of mixed Kru and German heritage. Her father was a lawyer whose family belonged to the Gola tribe. Ellen's biracial heritage and light skinned complexion was later used against her by political opponents.

Ellen grew up in a loving family in a close-knit community. She recalls that her block often felt more like an extended family than a neighborhood. As a child, she enjoyed playing sports with the boys in her neighborhood. Her friends and classmates often called her a "tomboy," but it never bothered her.

Ellen's father had a close relationship with President Tubman of Liberia, who sometimes visited her family's home with his entourage. During these times, her family would cook delicious Liberian food such as *fufu* (dumpling) with palm butter, meat stew, country chops, and *jollof rice*. These experiences helped Ellen to get a firsthand look at what it took to be a strong, authoritative leader from an early age.

> ❝ When the president arrived with all his government officials, we the children would be ushered into the background. We would peep around the corner to listen to their deep voices boom. ❞

Chapter 3

Education is Key

Education was important to Ellen's parents and the key to her success. Going to school meant the world to Ellen. From an early age she excelled in her studies and dreamt of becoming an English teacher, just like her mother. During her primary school years, Ellen's mother opened a school. It was close to Ellen's house and attended by many of her neighborhood friends.

After middle school, Ellen enrolled in the College of West Africa, one of the oldest and most prestigious high schools in Liberia. Though Ellen excelled in school, it wasn't an easy school to get into. Her father's position in the legislature and his connections had "opened the door" to attend the College of West Africa.

Here, she continued her love for sports. She played volleyball so well she was on her school's team. Ellen was a serious and assertive player who led her school team to win many games against rivals. Ellen loved school. Her only problem was that some of her classmates teased her about the fairness of her complexion.

> " They said I was too light to be a real African and called me Red Pumpkin, a name that hurt me to the bottom of my soul. Many days after school, I cried my way home. Many nights, I went to bed praying to God to let me wake black. It was the one wish I ever wanted in all my life, to wake up black. "

Chapter 4

Getting Married and Starting a Family

In her last year of high school, Ellen met a young man named James Sirleaf, affectionately known as "Doc." He'd recently returned to Liberia after studying agriculture at the Tuskegee Institute in the United States. Ellen and James had a lot in common and Ellen was swept off her feet. The couple decided to get married after Ellen completed high school.

Ellen graduated; she and James were married; Ellen took the combined surname Johnson Sirleaf; and the couple's first son, James Jr., was born the following year. Three more brothers followed and within five years of marriage, Ellen had become the mother of four young boys.

James had found a good job with the Department of Agriculture and Ellen supplemented their income by working as a bookkeeper. This sparked her interest in finance. Ellen had stepped into a role that would be the beginning of her career in finance. Ellen loved her family, but soon grew dissatisfied. She believed she wasn't living up to her potential. Something had to change.

> 66 Still once I took that position, I had stepped into a stream that would carry me along toward the future of my professional development. So often, it's the small decisions in life that end up shaping our future the most. 99

Chapter 5

Going to America

Ellen didn't have to wait long to find the change she was seeking. Doc was awarded a scholarship to continue his studies in agriculture in the United States. Ellen quickly seized the opportunity to further her own education.

After several attempts, she won a scholarship to pursue a degree in accounting. She followed her husband to the U.S. and the state of Wisconsin where she enrolled at Madison Business College. It was hard to leave her boys behind, but she was comforted by the fact that her family would take care of her boys.

Despite the cold Midwestern winters that were hard to get used to, Ellen adapted quickly to life in Wisconsin. She even grew to love American football. Cheering for her favorite team, the Green Bay Packers, she screamed until her voice faded to nothing but a whisper.

Sadly, Ellen's marriage was not a happy one. Doc often lost his temper and would hurt Ellen with his words and fists. His violence left a mark on her life and she was determined to do something about it. Ellen's family and friends were not surprised when she began to talk about divorcing Doc.

❝ One thing the western world can learn from traditional African culture is the awesome support of the extended family system. ❞

Chapter 6

Return to America and Back

Ellen returned to Liberia after completing her studies. She was thrilled to see her boys and continue her life as a mother. She soon took a job as director of the Treasury Department. There, she got a firsthand look at the nation's economy and learned it wasn't strong. This knowledge would serve her well in years to come.

Ellen found her role satisfying and continued to work and study, determined to advance her career. While her career soared, however, her marriage got worse. Ellen couldn't take any more abuse and sought a divorce from Doc.

In 1969, Ellen represented the Liberian Treasury Department at a conference organized by the Harvard Institute for International Development. She gave a fiery, unforgettable speech that touched a nerve with top officials in the Liberian government. She was advised to stay out of the country for her own safety. Ellen used this opportunity to further her studies.

> From my spot at the Treasury Department, I had a clear and unimpeded view of our nation's economy, and the view wasn't rosy.

Chapter 7

Life of Service in Government

Ellen once again returned to Liberia where she served as the assistant minister of Finance under President William Tolbert. Later, she served as the minister of finance in Samuel Doe's military government. In both cases, Ellen was responsible for national banking and finance policies. She became well known for her financial knowledge and personal integrity, even though she occasionally clashed with other government officials, including the two leaders she served.

In 1972, Ellen was invited by her alma mater, Harvard University, to give the graduation address. In her second speech at Harvard, Ellen used the podium to challenge the Liberian government in a way that could not be ignored. Members of the Liberian government were not pleased with Ellen's speech.

Knowing that she couldn't return to her position in Liberia, she accepted a job offer from the World Bank. Working on financial policies for several different countries, Ellen broadened and deepened her professional skill set. She returned to Liberia once again, this time as a World Bank official who assisted the government of Liberia.

In January 1985, Ellen openly criticized the military government and was sentenced to ten years in prison. In prison, Ellen learned more about the issues faced by ordinary citizens. She was later released following international pressure.

> " My release from prison shows the power of the public, the power of the people both home and abroad. Public opinion matters; if it is pointed, focused, and intense, it can turn things around. "

Chapter 8

The Civil Wars

The first of Liberia's two civil wars broke out in 1989. Ellen fled to the United States where she worked at Citibank. After a few years away, she returned to Liberia to run for vice president. However, she was removed from the ticket due to a speech where she criticized members of the government. Instead, she ran for a senate seat in the elections. Ellen won but refused to take her seat to protest election fraud.

The first civil war ended in 1997. After a short time of peace, the second civil war broke out in 1999 and lasted until 2003. The civil wars impacted massive numbers of families throughout the country. When the second civil war finally ended, 250,000 Liberians had been killed and almost one million displaced. Countries like Ghana and the United States took in thousands of Liberian refugees. Today, about 35,000 Liberians call the state of Minnesota home.

66 Monrovia was dubbed, 'the world's most dangerous place' by the international press. 99

Chapter 9

Route to Becoming President

Ellen campaigned for president in 1997 and lost to Charles Taylor. She was not deterred, however, and ran again in 2005. She took the lessons she'd learned from her first campaign and vowed to do better. She mobilized her "secret weapon," the women of Liberia, and sent them out to campaign for her.

Ellen's opponents used her mixed heritage against her. With partial European ancestry and a fairer complexion, some people argued that she was descended from the settler class. Therefore, they maintained, she couldn't understand the problems indigenous Africans faced. Ellen refuted this with a show of strength. With her mixed ancestry, she represented both worlds.

Other critics wanted to wipe the slate clean. They said Liberia needed a fresh new face who hadn't served in government before to help guide the country out of years of civil war. Ellen thought otherwise. She said the country needed someone with experience who could provide immediate leadership. She felt she was that person. Despite all the critics and doubters, Ellen continued to campaign very hard and won the hearts of the people.

> ❝ The odds were solidly against me, but I have always been the type of person who is determined to beat the odds. ❞

Chapter 10

Madam President

On November 23rd, against all odds, Ellen Johnson Sirleaf won the most votes and was declared the 23rd president of Liberia. Ellen was inaugurated into office on January 16th, 2006. She describes that day as euphoric.

It was a critical moment in the nation's history, and she broke the glass ceiling to become the first woman elected president in Africa. It was a moment seen around the world as one of hope and possibility. It seems like the wise elder who visited Ellen as a baby sensed something no one else saw. "This child shall be great," he said, and his prediction came true.

Ellen's greatness took her where no African woman had ever gone before. Ellen showed compassion and commitment. She fought for women's rights and advocated for education, justice and equality. Leading a nation run down by decades of civil war was a difficult task, but Ellen was determined to rebuild her nation. She became known internationally as, "Africa's Iron Lady."

❝ I felt a nearly overwhelming sense of pride in, and gratitude for thousands of Liberians who had supported me, especially the women. ❞

Chapter 11

Accomplishments

President Johnson led her nation with grit and perseverance in very difficult circumstances. Most importantly, she helped guide her country towards a peaceful and democratic future.

She accomplished a lot in office. Her notable achievements include:

- Seeing Liberia through reconciliation and recovery after the civil war that lasted ten years.
- Leading Liberia through the Ebola crisis.
- Securing millions of dollars of foreign investment. This was critical for Liberia because the country had just come out of two civil wars and needed money for reconstruction and governance.
- Increasing the national budget from $80 million to over $672 million during her time in office.
- Seeking private resources to rebuild schools, clinics and markets.
- Negotiating for about 4.6 billion U.S. dollars in loan forgiveness for Liberia.
- Negotiating to lift United Nations trade sanctions against Liberia.
- Establishing a Truth and Reconciliation Committee to deal with corruption and heal ethnic tensions in the country.

President Johnson has received many accolades and awards. These include the Nobel Peace Prize in 2011, the United States Presidential Medal of Freedom, and the Grand Croix of the Legion D' Honneur, France's highest public distinction. She was also named one of Forbes's 100 Most Powerful Women in the World.

Chapter 12

Ellen's Work Continues

Ma Ellen's work and its impact continues. In 2017, she was awarded the Ibrahim Prize For Achievement in African Leadership, becoming the first woman to receive this prize. She founded the Ellen Johnson Sirleaf Presidential Center for Women and Development. Ma Ellen broke several glass ceilings and is committed to ensuring other women break theirs too. Her latest endeavor is the Amujae Initiative, a program that inspires and prepares African women for roles in public leadership. She continues to be a tireless advocate for girls and women and currently serves as one of the Elders, an independent group of global leaders working together for peace and human rights.

> To girls and women everywhere, I issue a simple invitation. My sisters, my daughters, my friends; find your voice.

ABOUT THE AUTHOR

Rosemond Sarpong Owens is a diversity, equity and inclusion professional. She has a passion for history and storytelling and is inspired to share stories of changemakers of African descent.

Sarpong Owens is a wife and mother to three girls who love to read. She hopes that this book encourages children to be proud of themselves and their heritage.

References

Johnson Sirleaf, Ellen (2009). *This Child Will Be Great: Memoir of a Remarkable Life by Africa's First Woman President.* New York: HarperCollins.

https://www.ejscenter.org/about/ellen-johnson-sirleaf/
Retrieved June, 2021.

https://www.un.org/en/conf/migration/assets/pdf/Ellen-Sirleaf-Bio.pdf
Retrieved, April, 2021

"The Nobel Peace Prize 2011". *NobelPrize.org.*
Retrieved March 2021.

https://www.britannica.com/biography/Ellen-Johnson-Sirleaf
Retrieved, April, 2021

ACKNOWLEDGEMENTS

For her support of this book, thanks to Her Excellency Jewel Taylor, Vice President of Liberia.

For his work on editing this book, thanks to John Schaidler.

For her work on and support of this book, thanks to Letitia deGraft Okyere.

Other Books in the Heritage Collection

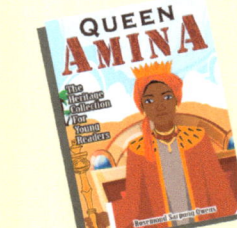

The story of Queen Amina is an important one for girls everywhere. Explore how Queen Amina gained a reputation as a fearless warrior, breaking barriers at a time when men dominated most aspects of life. Queen Amina's life will inspire and encourage you to be fearless.

Who was Queen Nandi? She is referred to as one of the greatest mothers that ever lived. As a queen mother, she saw her son Shaka become one of the greatest kings of the Zulu people and builder of the Zulu empire. Read her story and learn how she made her mark in history.

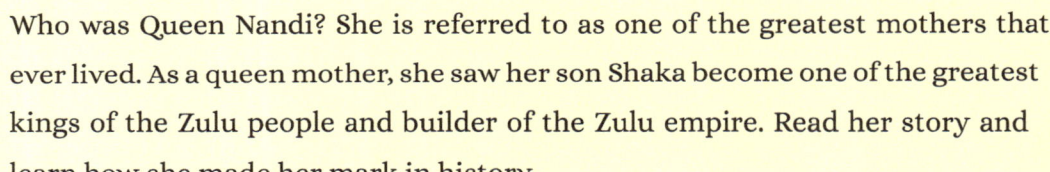

Eléni was a princess from Hadiya who became the wife of Emperor Zara Yaqob in 1445. Eléni guided the reign of five emperors and fearlessly challenged the leading role men played in society as an empress, queen mother and regent. Eléni's story will inspire girls and women everywhere to rise above difficult circumstances and fulfill their destiny.

R.J. Ghartey saw no limits to what he could achieve. As a young man, he rejected traditional paths of fishing and farming and learned a different trade. Through this, he became an influential business entrepreneur. In addition, Ghartey played an important role in local politics and found ways to improve the lives of those in his community. In telling Ghartey's story, the author hopes to encourage children with different dreams to pursue their destinies past challenges that they may face.